▸ Agriculture ▸ Energy ▾ **Entertainment Industry** ▸ Environment & Sustainability

▸ Forensics ▸ Information Technology ▸ Medicine and Health Care

▸ Space Science ▸ Transportation ▸ War and the Military

# ENTERTAINMENT INDUSTRY

Digital Transmission

Virtual Reality Entertainment

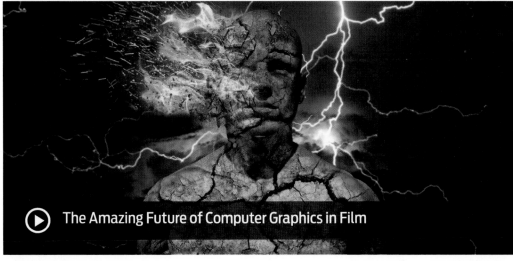

The Amazing Future of Computer Graphics in Film

## STEM IN CURRENT EVENTS

Agriculture

Energy

Entertainment Industry

Environment & Sustainability

Forensics

Information Technology

Medicine and Health Care

Space Science

Transportation

War and the Military

# STEM IN CURRENT EVENTS

# ENTERTAINMENT INDUSTRY

## By Michael Centore

MASON CREST

## Mason Crest
450 Parkway Drive, Suite D
Broomall, PA 19008
www.masoncrest.com

© 2017 by Mason Crest, an imprint of National Highlights, Inc.

Printed and bound in the United States of America.

First printing
9 8 7 6 5 4 3 2 1

Series ISBN: 978-1-4222-3587-4
ISBN: 978-1-4222-3590-4
ebook ISBN: 978-1-4222-8291-5

Produced by Shoreline Publishing Group
*Designer:* Tom Carling, Carling Design Inc.
*Production:* Sandy Gordon
www.shorelinepublishing.com

Front cover: Dreamstime.com: Phudui tl; Innovatedcaptures tr; Activedia b.

Library of Congress Cataloging-in-Publication Data

Names: Centore, Michael, 1980- Title: Entertainment industry / by Michael Centore.
Description: Broomall, PA : Mason Crest, [2017] |
Series: STEM in current   events | Includes index.
Identifiers: LCCN 2016004738| ISBN 9781422235904 (hardback) | ISBN   9781422235874 (series) | ISBN
    9781422282915 (ebook)
Subjects: LCSH: Entertainment events--Juvenile literature. | Animal   trainers--Juvenile literature. | Computer
    graphics--Juvenile literature. |   Television broadcasting--Special effects--Juvenile literature. |
    Circus--Juvenile literature.
Classification: LCC GV45 .C46 2017 | DDC 790.1--dc23
LC record available at http://lccn.loc.gov/2016004738

# Contents

Introduction: That's Entertainment! ........................................6

**1** Science and Entertainment ...............................8

**2** Technology and Entertainment ........................20

**3** Engineering and Entertainment ......................34

**4** Math and Entertainment ................................50

Find Out More............................................................62

Series Glossary of Key Terms......................................63

Index/Author .............................................................64

## Key Icons to Look For

 **Words to Understand:** These words with their easy-to-understand definitions will increase the reader's understanding of the text, while building vocabulary skills.

 **Sidebars:** This boxed material within the main text allows readers to build knowledge, gain insights, explore possibilities, and broaden their perspectives by weaving together additional information to provide realistic and holistic perspectives.

 **Educational Videos**: Readers can view videos by scanning our QR codes, providing them with additional educational content to supplement the text. Examples include news coverage, moments in history, speeches, iconic sports moments, and much more!

 **Text-Dependent Questions:** These questions send the reader back to the text for more careful attention to the evidence presented here.

 **Research Projects:** Readers are pointed toward areas of further inquiry connected to each chapter. Suggestions are provided for projects that encourage deeper research and analysis.

 **Series Glossary of Key Terms:** This back-of-the-book glossary contains terminology used throughout this series. Words found here increase the reader's ability to read and comprehend higher-level books and articles in this field.

# INTRODUCTION

# That's Entertainment!

We often hear of technological advances in the entertainment industry. Things like digital movie projection, new ways of streaming and sharing music, and the rise of computer-generated animation are relatively recent developments that have changed the way media are produced and consumed. It seems that as soon as one technology evolves, another takes its place. Software is constantly being updated; new apps and hardware such as Kindles and iPads get sleeker and more powerful by the year. With this comes an ability to experience more entertainment content than ever before.

The other elements of STEM, however—science, engineering, and math—don't seem to have as much to do with the entertainment industry at first glance. The worlds of film and music make us think of creative types coming up with intricate stories or lyrics to songs; rarely do we picture them conducting experiments or solving equations. But a closer look shows that entertainment professionals of all kinds rely on STEM to get their jobs done.

In this book we'll take a look at how a few of these professionals are using STEM, as well as some of the cutting-edge inventions that are moving the industry forward. We'll see how an understanding of the physics of light has impacted 3D movies; learn how engineers design giant moving stage sets for theatrical productions and rig intricate wire systems so actors can fly over crowds; take a spin on some of the world's most advanced roller coasters and waterslides, some powered by the latest in magnetic levitation technology; and discover how mathematical algorithms are revolutionizing the way book, movie, and music sales are tracked—and even how songs and movies are produced.

The natural sciences, too, are alive and well in the entertainment industry. We'll get a close-up look at the ways insect wranglers and animal handlers use biology and behavioral science to train nonhuman "actors" on set, and find out about the always-desirable

Going to the movies has always been a technology-based experience. Today, however, new advances in science and tech are making all forms of entertainment amazing!

job of film science consulting. We'll also look at some of the ethical issues that come up in the wake of scientific breakthroughs, such as how digital body scans could one day replace live human actors. From the audience side, we'll check out a state-of-the-art 4DX multisensory movie theater complete with rumbling chairs and a rain simulator.

Of course, the entertainment industry isn't the only field in which innovation and creativity are pushing the boundaries of what's possible. From the environmental sciences to the energy sector to sports, breakthroughs based in STEM subjects are opening the possibilities for a more connected, efficient, and sustainable planet.

While the scientific principles that govern our physical world are unchanging, those with the curiosity and daringness to imagine new applications for them are leading the way to the future. The entertainment industry, with its combination of creative and scientific thinking, is a great lens through which to view these new developments.

On the set of a film that uses animals, experts in animal behavior and biology called "wranglers" are responsible for the care—and the acting—of the nonhuman cast members.

# SCIENCE AND
# Entertainment

## Words to Understand

**behavioral science**   the study of how humans and animals behave as they are observed in the wild or in controlled environments

**computer-generated imagery**   the use of computer graphics to create special effects

**entomologist**   a person who studies insects

**ethical**   a behavior that is seen as good and decent

**inclinations**   tendencies to act a certain way

**perennial**   something that happens frequently

## Animal Wranglers

**C**hances are you've seen a movie or TV show where an animal, insect, or other critter has played a prominent role. From classic programs like *Lassie*, which tells the story of a young boy's friendship with his trustworthy collie, to science-fiction films such as *The Swarm*, where thousands of killer bees invade the state of Texas, tales of humans' interactions with other species are **perennial** choices for entertaining plotlines. Of course, these nonhuman creatures don't just act naturally—they have to be guided. That is where insect wranglers and animal handlers come in.

An insect wrangler is a person, often an **entomologist**, who is trained to work with bugs. Insect wranglers not only direct all manner of cockroaches, maggots, spiders, and other species on movie sets, but they also breed and store them. If a director wants a specific type of insect that's not readily available, it's the wrangler's job to track it down. That may mean visiting other breeders in far-off places.

Meet a Hollywood animal wrangler.

On set, insect wranglers must use their scientific knowledge about the behavior of bugs. For example, recognizing that cockroaches seek out enclosed spaces can help a wrangler construct a course to get them to move along a certain path. Understanding their life cycles—the season in which they're born, how long they live, and other related facts—is necessary when breeding different species. On a purely health-related level, knowing which bugs are more likely to carry diseases or cause allergies is necessary to keep a cast and crew safe. Even the insects' diets must be closely monitored to ensure they haven't been feeding on bacteria.

Safety isn't just a human concern. Some insects must be washed, and they must be kept away from potentially toxic environments such as freshly painted rooms. Insects have to be stored in particular ways, in temperature-controlled spaces to mimic their natural habitats. Transport to and from the set presents its own challenges; wranglers may have to design special containers to prevent against infestation. They may also have to separate insects by sex to make sure they don't reproduce.

*Animals in the movies are not just dogs and cats. This film from Thailand is using an elephant, handled by the animal wrangler in front, who also appears in the film.*

On a slightly larger scale, animal handlers work with everything from reptiles to horses to chickens, training them for appearances on camera and ensuring they're properly cared for. Handlers have to understand animal behavior, diet, and even social **inclinations**. Some of them have worked with the same animals for years to learn how they think and act. Like insect wranglers, handlers are often responsible for housing and caring for their own animals. That might include re-creating their natural habitats and providing them with special food, such as mice for snakes.

The field of animal handling, however, is changing. One reason is an increased awareness of animal rights in the film industry and beyond. News of animals that have died or been injured

## Tricks of the Trade

Insect wranglers have developed many tried-and-true strategies for getting insects to act in certain ways. Lines of sugar laid out in certain patterns can get ants to march in formation; a quick stint in a cooler can slow down a mosquito just long enough for a close-up; and a tiny bit of honey will force a fly to clean itself. Sometimes the wranglers have to make up things on the spot, problem-solving according to the whims of a director or the logistics of filming. Butterflies are most active during the daylight hours, for instance, but if the crew isn't ready until nightfall, the wranglers have to improvise.

during film productions have led some people to question whether animal-handling practices are **ethical**; some say that the animals are exploited and are bred and raised in poor conditions. Over the years, handlers have responded to these concerns with new training practices based in **behavioral science**, such as motivating animals with positive reinforcement rather than forcing them aggressively to do certain things.

## Physics of CGI

When it comes to science-fiction and fantasy films, live-action cinematography sometimes just doesn't do the trick. The 2009 movie *Avatar*, for example, depended heavily on computer technologies such as motion capture (a means of digitally recording human movement for use in computer animations) to render its otherworldly characters and alien environments. What many people *don't* realize is just how much physics goes into this sort of **computer-generated imagery** (CGI).

Since CGI does not use traditional artists to draw and animate different scenes, physicists help computer animators calculate movement with various equations. By simulating the ways that solids and fluids move in the real world, they can create highly realistic images of drifting smoke, flickering fire, windswept hair, and other objects. According to one CGI physicist, water is one of the hardest to depict realistically, since its surface geometry is always shifting. Physics-based CGI is less expensive than live-action filming and is safer for casts and crews—especially when scenes call for high-risk stunts or settings.

The physics of film doesn't just end in production; it carries on to you, the viewer, in experiences like 3D movies. The technology behind 3D screening dates to the 19th century, when English scientist Sir Charles Wheatstone demonstrated how humans see in three dimensions by "fusing" together images taken in by each eye separately. This is referred to as stereoscopic vision. Three-dimensional films build on this process by recording images with

A digital drawing pad like this one is used by many computer graphics artists. The stylus transfers the lines the artist makes into digital files that can be manipulated on screen.

Not quite stylish enough for the street, 3D glasses like these are perfect to wear in a darkened theater, as surprisingly old technology is played out in new films.

two separate lenses, much like human eyes. In the 3D movies of yesteryear, one of these lenses was filtered with red and the other with blue. When the viewer wore a special set of red and blue glasses, one eye let in the red light and the other the blue light from the film. The result was that each eye combined its own perspective into a 3D image.

The problem with this old-fashioned method was that filmmakers couldn't use a full spectrum of color. Today's 3D movies are much more sophisticated. They use something called polarized light to create a 3D effect *and* preserve color and clarity of image.

Polarized light is light that vibrates along a single plane. In contrast, the sun's light is unpolarized, meaning that it vibrates across many different planes. The process of turning unpolarized light into polarized light is called polarization. There are different methods of polarization, but the most common is with a polaroid filter. This is the method used in making modern 3D movies. The film is shot using two lenses, and when it is screened, two projectors are used: the left one polarizes the light in one direction, and the right one polarizes the light in the other. Viewers wear glasses with polarizing filters as well; the left lens blocks the light oriented for the right eye and vice versa, and the brain registers the image three-dimensionally.

The most cutting-edge 3D technology features digital cameras that incorporate both lenses into a single device, and digital projectors that can project both sets of images out of a single lens. They do this by alternating between the left-eye and right-eye frames an astonishing 144 times per second. Instead of linear polarity, which is when the light is oriented either horizontally or vertically, these new systems use rotational polarity, where the light is oriented in circles. The principle is the same as with linear polarity: The light for one eye spins clockwise, the light for the other counterclockwise, and the viewer's polarized glasses "decode" these rotations to register a 3D image.

# Getting the Science Right

To make sure all those far-out stories you're seeing projected up on the silver screen are scientifically accurate, Hollywood producers will hire science consultants. These are men and women trained

## Ahead of His Time

Though nearly 50 years old, *2001: A Space Odyssey*—American director Stanley Kubrick's science fiction epic—is still the measure for the role of science consulting in film. Kubrick's consultancy team included two former NASA scientists and some 65 science-related companies, governmental organizations, and research groups. The most intensive effort went into accurately rendering the *Discovery One*, the fictional nuclear-powered spaceship in the movie. Consultants also helped to realistically portray outer space as being totally silent, the visual effects of weightlessness in space, and even the delays in communication between the spaceship and Earth because of the vast distance separating them.

in all sorts of scientific disciplines, from astrophysics to engineering to chemistry. They advise screenwriters and directors on the science-related parts of their movies. Often these consultants are top academics taking a break from the rigors of teaching and research. They may not get paid much (if at all), but the "cool factor" of working on a major motion picture or television show—not to mention the joy of introducing scientific concepts to audiences all over the world—is often enough to attract their services.

Scientific consultants have worked with the *Spider-Man* movie franchise to analyze the physics behind the superhero's climbing powers, the television show *The Big Bang Theory* to "punch up" the scientific dialogue between characters to make it more realistic, and the movie *Thor* to create (somewhat) more probable explanations for the main character's journey through space and time. While consultants admit that entertainment value is the chief concern for a Hollywood blockbuster, they are proud to help enrich the plotline with insightful, authentic scientific details.

# The Science of Dance

Many structures of the entertainment world, from elaborate stage sets to camera cranes and dollies, use physics to achieve their aims. But what about the human body itself? In the field of dance, one of the most ancient forms of human expression and entertainment, physical laws are constantly at play. Over the past several years, dancers and physicists have worked together to explore the relationship between the two. Their work has given dancers a deeper understanding of their craft.

One physics principle that dancers are familiar with is the center of mass. It is the point in an object where all mass is concentrated, holding the object in perfect balance. In the human body, the center of mass is right below the stomach in the pelvic region. Its location keeps the body upright. However, as a dancer spins, she must work to keep the center of mass directly above her feet so she doesn't stumble or fall over. This can be especially difficult in dance forms such as ballet, where motion should appear fluid and the audience should not see the dancer correcting herself. Center of mass is also crucial for executing the ballet leap known as grand jeté. To create the illusion of floating through space, the dancer lifts her legs to raise her center of mass at the peak of her leap. By keeping her center of mass as still as possible, she appears to be "hovering" in midair.

Momentum and torque are other physics concepts important to dancers. Momentum is the movement of mass; it is measured by the amount of mass times the speed at which it is moving. Linear momentum is movement in a line. Dancers must learn to control their linear momentum as they move across a stage. Turns have their own set of physical principles: angular velocity (how fast an object rotates); rotational inertia (the tendency of a spinning object to keep on spinning); and angular momentum (like linear momentum, only measuring rotating movement). Torque is the amount of force applied to an object to get it to turn. The more torque that is applied, the stronger the angular momentum of the turn. One way a dancer may apply torque is by pushing off against the floor.

To study the ways that physics impact dance performance, researchers and students at Denison University in Ohio have set up an electronic laboratory with six 3D cameras, three laptops, and 70 wearable motion-capture reflectors to track movement and render it digitally. Researchers can study the ways that a dancer's center of mass moves in relation to the floor, the angles of the limbs as they turn and leap, and other details. At Yale,

*Physics students at work? Actually . . . yes. Dancers have to have a good understanding of the physical laws of movement and motion to perform their amazing feats.*

dancers have used advanced scientific concepts such as particle physics as inspiration for choreography. Dancers say this kind of interdisciplinary approach has led to more imaginative pieces, while physicists appreciate being able to show the creative side of their field and find new applications for their research.

 ## Text-Dependent Questions

1. What are three elements of an insect wrangler's job?

2. How have animal handlers responded to claims that training methods are unethical?

3. What is the difference between polarized and unpolarized light, and what is the most common method of polarization?

 ## Research Project

Find a film you enjoy with scientific themes—anything from a superhero movie to a science-fiction story. Watch the film while pretending you are a science consultant. List the elements of the film that you think are accurate and those you think are inaccurate or hard to believe. Based on your knowledge of science, write a brief "report" to the director explaining what you felt worked, what didn't, and how you might go about making things more authentic.

This announcer sits in front of a green screen, but to the viewers at home, he could look like he is sitting anywhere in the world . . . real or not!

# TECHNOLOGY AND
# Entertainment

## Words to Understand

**autonomous**   having the ability to act independently

**contrasts**   differs from

**humane**   marked by compassion and consideration

**multisensory**   involving more than one of the five senses

**proponents**   people who are in favor of something

**revitalizing**   giving new life to something

## Green Screens

Fifty years ago, if the script of a Hollywood Western called for a horse to topple over, it was not uncommon for animal handlers to set up a wire—the animal would run across the frame, unaware, until it tripped and fell. Such cruel and unusual methods have fallen out of favor today, as people's attitudes toward animals have evolved and training practices have become more **humane**. Advances in technology have contributed to this trend. New developments in chromakey, or "green-screen" technology, for example, have made it easier for handlers to "direct" animals without pushing them unfairly.

The concept of chromakey is fairly simple: If something is filmed in front of a single-color backdrop, computer software can be used to make that color transparent. Any image can be used to replace it—a particular landscape, a video, or whatever else the filmmaker has in mind. One of the most well-known uses for chromakey technology occurs every night during the evening news. Though the weatherman appears to be standing in front of a map, it is actually a computerized image replacing a green screen behind him. While any color can be used for the screen, bright green is the most common because it **contrasts** strikingly

Green screens can be as small as this portable set or as large as a warehouse-size soundstage used for superhero movies. They are lit and filmed at any size.

with the people in front of it. This makes it easier to separate out the background and insert a new one.

Inside the basics of chroma key tech

Chromakey technology has many uses in the film world, where movies often call for supernatural special effects. It allows directors to put actors in otherwise impossible (or at least hard-to-shoot) situations, from wandering around an ancient city to flying through outer space. In recent years, the technology has been adopted by the animal handling industry. Handlers film all sorts of different animals in front of green screens, recording their movements and sounds. The clips are filed away in a digital library and licensed to film production companies, who can then alter the backgrounds in whatever way they see fit.

**Proponents** of animal green-screening cite many advantages. One is how much money it saves, since production companies don't need to hire trainers or transport animals onto sets. Since the clips are easily searchable, it also saves time: directors and editors can browse through them, pick the ones they need, and put them into production right away. But beyond the business aspects, the technology has benefits for the animals. There is less chance of injury in a green-screen studio than there is outside on set. Animals are not under pressure to perform a scene in a fixed amount of time, as they often are on big-budget movies where every minute costs money. This reduces their stress levels and respects their limitations, making for a healthier, safer environment.

## Getting Your Guffaws' Worth

If you've ever been to a comedy film or stand-up performance and felt you overpaid, you might appreciate a recent technological development that's helping audiences get their money's worth. At the Teatreneu club in Barcelona, Spain, facial-recognition tablets are installed into the back of every seat. The tablets use special software to track a person's expression throughout a comedy show. Every time the tablet registers a laugh, the audience member is charged 0.3 euros (or about US$0.33), with a limit of about US$25.75. The technology was introduced to increase audience numbers, which had dwindled due to new government taxes on theater tickets. Other clubs in Spain, France, and Finland have been incorporating the software, and the Teatreneu recently introduced a "pay-per-laugh" season ticket to generate repeat customers.

Chromakey is far from the only computer-based technology **revitalizing** the entertainment world. Computer-generated imagery (CGI) has a whole host of applications, from making animated movies more lifelike to creating realistic-looking fractal landscapes (more on these in chapter 4). It is also having a profound impact on the future of actors and acting.

## Animating People

Motion-capture technology has allowed actors to portray nonhuman characters with astounding realism and directors to enhance human ones with digital effects. Two of the most common methods of motion capture are optical-passive and optical-active. In optical-passive, an actor wears special reflective markers at various points on his or her body. Infrared cameras track the movements of the markers. There may be anywhere from two to more than 50 cameras working together to gather and process the actor's coordinates. Later, animators take the recorded data and apply it to computer-generated characters, which makes their movements more fluid and realistic. In optical-active capture, the actor wears a suit wired with LED markers. (LED stands for

Technology is one of the few ways to capture NHL star Alexander Ovechkin. He wore motion-capture lights to have his movements "captured" for use in a video game.

"light-emitting diode," which converts electric current directly into light.) Instead of reflecting light back to the cameras, these LED suits generate their own.

The 2014 film *Dawn of the Planet of the Apes* introduced new challenges to motion capture. Since most of the movie was shot outdoors, away from light-controlled studio environments, passive reflective markers were unreliable—even with almost 60 cameras tracking the actors' movements. LED markers were good for short-term filming, but could not hold up during the long, involved takes in unpredictable weather. The crew responded by encasing the LED markers in hard plastic strips and making them remote controlled—they could be dimmed or brightened depending on changing conditions, even as the actors were filming their scenes. Data captured by the cameras was saved and sent to a team of animators, who could use it as the basic structure for their digital characters.

A variation on motion capture is facial performance capture. This is when the subtle facial expressions of actors are recorded and digitized. Facial motion capture either uses marker-based or markerless technology. Marker-based technology is similar to full-body motion-capture methods in that cameras track the movements of markers affixed to an actor's face. There may be more than 300 markers placed along the lips, eyes, nostrils, and other areas where motion is most prominent. Markerless technology first takes a scan of the actor's face in a neutral position. His or her movements are measured as they deviate from the neutral position, tracking them frame by frame.

Related to performance capture is 3D image scanning. This is a technique that is slowly changing the way films are cast. An actor's face is scanned using multiple cameras, registering its shape and curvature. From this information, specialists can create a "digital double" of the actor that can be used in later films. This opens up whole new avenues of film production. In the near future, anyone may be able to cull through a "library" of scanned actors and make movies using their likenesses. Actors with smaller parts or "extras" with background roles could feasibly be drawn from digital archives in order to keep production costs down. Even actors who have passed away could still "act" in films, provided their images have been scanned. This actually happened during production of the 2015 movie *Furious 7*. After lead actor Paul Walker died tragically in a car accident, his computer-generated image was used to complete the movie.

Making these scans even more lifelike are new technologies that allow computer scientists to re-create the movement of human skin. They do this by zooming in on small patches of skin as it is

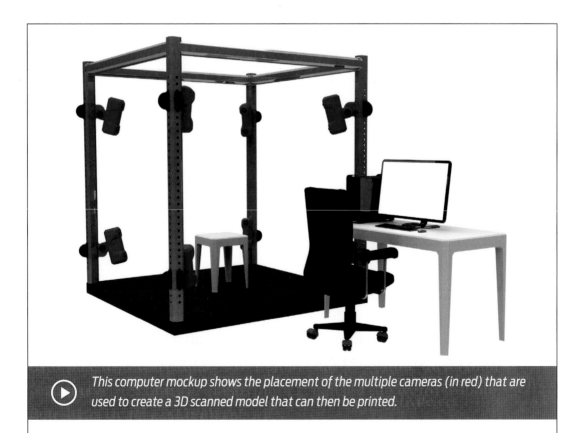

This computer mockup shows the placement of the multiple cameras (in red) that are used to create a 3D scanned model that can then be printed.

*Virtual reality headsets like these might be how we all watch movies in the future. They fully immerse a person's vision into whatever "reality" is being shown on the screen.*

manipulated by a special device. A camera tracks and captures its slightest movements down to the changing shape of the pores.

Eventually, computer scientists would like to put all these things together and create **autonomous** virtual actors who can respond to cues. While the technology for this is still a long ways off, the entertainment industry continues to rely more and more on computer-generated imagery. Actors who have been scanned must be aware of how their digital likenesses are being used by production studios. It may be that one day these likenesses—and not the actors themselves—are the ones cast in movies.

# Changing How We See Movies

When it comes time to watch Hollywood productions, viewers aren't limited by old-fashioned theaters anymore. Even the latest advances in 3D technology (see chapter 1) are now rivaled by 4DX and virtual-reality cinema. The former is an immersive, **multisensory** movie-going experience in which screenings are enhanced with physical effects. These are perfectly timed to the action of the film—chairs rumble and shake, air blows onto the audience to mimic wind, water falls from the ceiling during an onscreen rainstorm. Theaters are even equipped to fill the air with various scents. The technology works by having a distinct 4DX "track" layered atop the film's audio and video tracks. Separate 4DX "editors" create this track by putting together different effects to sync with the movie. To date, there are more than 200 4DX cinemas worldwide; the first one in the United States opened in Los Angeles in 2014.

The most cutting-edge viewing experience (and the one that is still largely in development) is virtual-reality cinema. It is where the viewer wears a virtual-reality headset complete with

## Emotion Capture

There is a movement in the entertainment industry to begin recognizing motion-capture actors and actresses more openly for their work. Many professionals felt Andy Serkis, who provided the real-life movements for the computerized chimpanzee Caesar in *Dawn of the Planet of the Apes*, deserved an Oscar nomination for his ability to enliven the character. Another motion-capture actor named Woody Schultz wrote a column for *The New York Times* describing what it feels like to be the person behind so many memorable movie characters and yet still unknown by the general public. He describes the unique collaboration between the actor, who gives the character its internal shape and substance, and the animator, who provides its external appearance. This partnership is still very new in the history of film, with creative possibilities that have only begun to be explored.

## Theater in the Round

Films aren't the only medium working with virtual reality. The famed theatrical production company Cirque du Soleil (read more about their engineering feats in the next chapter) is creating a show called *KURIOS (Cabinet of Curiosities)*. Audience members wear virtual-reality headsets and are completely immersed in the plot of the story, which revolves around an inventor and his "cabinet of curiosities." The technology was developed in collaboration with an electronics company and a film studio. The studio created special cameras with multiple lenses and microphones to pick up full 360-degree views and sound. Filming the characters is one thing, but the real challenge comes in the editing stage—filmmakers must piece together footage from many different angles into a coherent whole.

high-resolution lenses, a 360-degree positional tracking system that uses sensors to follow the movement of the head, and built-in headphones for audio in order to watch a film. The few movies that have been produced for virtual-reality headsets take advantage of the "first-person" nature of the technology—the viewer becomes an active participant in the film, guiding the direction of the story. Characters may or may not appear depending on whether viewers turn to take them in; sounds and dialogue change depending on how they tilt their heads. The first commercially available virtual-reality headset, which should widen the audience for this new wave of filmmaking, is scheduled to appear in 2016.

## Iron Man or Plastic Man?

When we think of a printer, the first thing that comes to mind is probably ink and paper. Traditional household and office printers are used to transfer images and text from a computer screen onto a physical page. But new technological developments in 3D printing are changing the ways we think about what printers are and what they can accomplish—and the entertainment industry is taking note. In brief, 3D printers are machines that can produce complete objects—not just images and text—from computer files. The process begins when a programmer virtually renders an object with a computer-aided design (CAD) program. She specifies the height, length, width, and other features to create a file. If she is not creating a new object, but instead looking to reproduce an existing object, she might use a 3D scanner. 3D scanners employ the latest in laser technologies to "copy" objects and create printable CAD files.

Whether the file is an original or a scanned design, the next step is to send it to the 3D printer. It works by adding layer upon layer of material, such as plastic, resin, nylon, and others, until the object is fully formed. The layers can be as thin as 16 microns—less than the width of a human hair! That control allows for very specific nuances in object design.

Such printing has found many applications in both the film and gaming industries, not to mention the fields of architecture, fashion design, and medicine. In the film *Iron Man 2*, for instance, the suit worn by star Robert Downey Jr. was created using 3D modeling and printing techniques. The main advantage of 3D printing is that it allows designers to make modifications to an object without having to rebuild it from scratch every time. In big-budget Hollywood movies, that can save considerable time and money. With *Iron Man 2*, for instance, designers were able to print smaller versions of the suit, give it to the director and producers to review, incorporate their adjustments, and reprint the updated file.

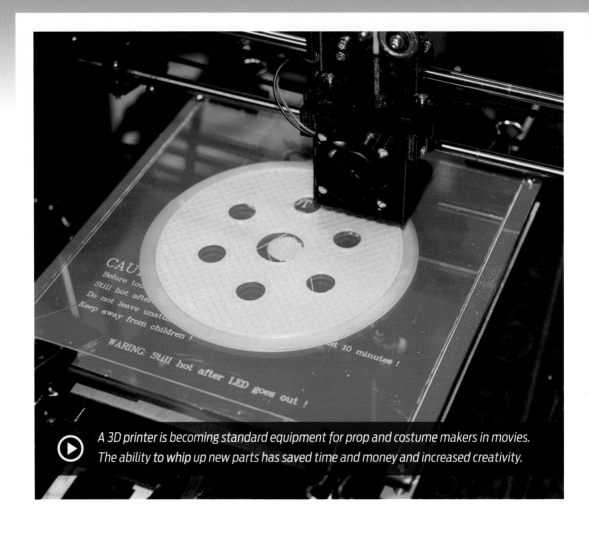

A 3D printer is becoming standard equipment for prop and costume makers in movies. The ability to whip up new parts has saved time and money and increased creativity.

The 3D printer that created the costume used a special type of powdered plastic sealed with UV light and coated with a thin layer of paint. Because of the printer's precision, the suit was able to be custom fitted to the actor and was not as heavy as a traditionally designed costume. That led to more realistic performances in the film. Also, if separate suits were needed for stuntmen, designers were able to make necessary tweaks in a short amount of time.

As newer, stronger printable materials are developed, it will open the door to more advanced uses of the technology. Medical specialists are already able to print customized knee replacements for their patients, while the ability to print human cells for tissue and organ transplants may soon become a reality. Since the entertainment industry is at the forefront of 3D printing, designers are often asked to share their knowledge with professionals in other fields, from aerospace to athletics. That type of research ensures that the future of 3D printing will continue to expand.

 **Text-Dependent Questions**

1. What are some uses of chromakey technology?

2. How do optical-passive and optical-active methods of motion capture differ?

3. How might 3D image scanning change the way movies are cast?

 **Research Project**

Research a new or important technological development in an entertainment medium not covered in this chapter, such as music or video games. Write a summary describing this development, how it works, key figures in its creation, and how it's impacting the entertainment world.

The future of movies: Inside 4DX technology

The performers at Cirque de Soleil's Ká dance, move, jump, and leap on top of a high-tech, mobile, platform-based stage that is a marvel of entertainment engineering.

# ENGINEERING AND
# Entertainment

## Words to Understand

**gravitational force**  a force acting on a body due to acceleration or gravity at the Earth's surface

**hydraulic**  describing something operated by fluid forced through a pressurized space

**inertia**  the resistance of an object to changing speed unless acted upon by an external force

**opulent**  extremely fancy or costly

**winch**  a device for lifting made of a rope or cable wound around a rotating drum and turned by a crank or other power source

## Engineering the Circus

The entertainment company Cirque du Soleil, founded in 1984 by two former street performers in Montreal, Canada, has grown to become the world's largest theatrical producer. Fifteen million people saw a Cirque du Soleil show in 2014 alone, in locations all over the world. By far one of its most popular is the coming-of-age tale *Kà*, a resident production at the MGM Grand hotel and casino in Las Vegas.

The seats at top right are at the stage level. The massive staging structure beneath that level rises up and down, depending on the needs of the performance.

*Kà* is believed to be the one of the most **opulent** theatrical productions in history. Eighty performers plus hundreds of other crew members are involved. The centerpiece of the show, however—and one of the feats of modern-day entertainment engineering—is the gigantic moving stage known as the "Sand Cliff deck." The Sand Cliff deck is one of seven stages used in the production. It is 25 by 50 feet (7.6 x 15.2 m) and weighs a whopping 150 tons. This would be a spectacle in itself, but the Sand Cliff's wide range of movements—including tilting to a 100-degree angle and rotating 360 degrees—put it over the top.

The engineering behind the Sand Cliff deck is a performance in itself. A custom-made, freestanding 300,000-pound (136,000 kg) gantry crane outfitted with special motion control machinery is attached to the stage. The crane is powered by **hydraulic** cylinders that lift the stage 70 feet (21.3 m) from the basement below. In an environmentally friendly move, the show's engineers opted to use vegetable oil instead of another hydraulic oil to drive the cylinders. Five piston pumps process 650 gallons (2,460 l) of the vegetable oil per minute. While these pumps were originally designed for industrial use, engineers working with the show's producers preferred them for their low noise level. This let them make the desired technical advances while considering the audience's needs as well.

Another theatrical show with an involved engineering setup is the touring production *Marvel Universe LIVE!* In the show, different characters from the worlds of Marvel Comics "come alive" in front of 3D projections and other video effects to perform all kinds of stunts. Where shows such as *Kà* focus their engineering efforts on stage construction and design, *Marvel Universe* requires complicated riggings, or systems of ropes and cables, to move characters and props through the air. Adding to the complexity is the fact that these riggings must be taken down and reinstalled in each new venue.

For the show, engineers designed two **winch** "farms," or groups of six winches attached to a frame. There is a "farm" on either side of the stage. Lines attached to each of the winches can couple with lines dropping from an overhanging scaffold. Each of the 12 winches has its own operator. The operator is in charge of enabling and disabling the winch and clipping it to the proper hanging line. Once the winch is securely fastened to the line, a performer can be raised; once the performer is raised, the operator can release the winch so that the performer can be controlled from an automated desk in another part of the theater. Using a state-of-the-art computerized system, the person behind the desk can direct the performer's flight path, from swooping in and out of the theatrical space to gliding over the audience.

## Fast-Moving Thrills

Such effects are definitely a thrill to *watch*—but what about events where you are allowed to *participate*? Engineers work to provide you with exciting entertainment adventures in places like theme parks or water parks. Roller coaster engineers specialize in designing, constructing, and testing all types of roller coasters. They select the materials, such as type of track, and perform all the calculations necessary to plan a thrilling, yet safe, ride.

Roller-coaster testing is an involved process. Engineers must tweak speeds and forces to ensure the human body can withstand them. For instance, if a person experiences five units of **gravitational force** (one unit is defined as 9.8 meters per second squared) for longer

### Custom Acoustics

Different types of music sound better in different types of environments. Classical music, for example, sounds best in concert halls without much on the walls to absorb sound. This way the music is allowed to reverberate, or echo, for a longer period of time, giving it a clearer tone. Rock music, which is often electrically amplified, sounds better in a more insulated space to absorb some of the reverberation. The problem is, most concert halls have to host both, and customizing the environment for every show is very hard to do—until now. A Danish drummer and sound specialist has designed inflatable membranes that can change the amount of reverberation in a room. The membranes are made of a special plastic foil and raised to ceilings or walls. When inflated, they absorb more reverberation, and when deflated, they absorb less. Concert halls can open their schedules to all types of performances and trust they'll have quality sound.

Before anyone climbs aboard a new roller coaster, extensive testing is done with empty cars (shown) and even with cars filled with dummies or sandbags.

than five seconds, he or she will probably lose consciousness. Loops, embankments, and other "extras" add further challenges. Engineers might also be constrained by the planned location of the coaster or the amount of money a park has to spend.

Roller-coaster technology continues to advance. One development that has considerably changed the engineering of coasters is the use of linear induction motors (LIMs) or linear synchronous motors (LSMs) to launch, drive, and brake instead of traditional methods like chain lifts. Linear motors use electromagnets to

Seriously? Only the brave will take on this challenge, the world's highest waterslide at a park in Kansas City. Engineers had to ensure both thrills and safety.

create two magnetic fields, one on the tracks and the other on the bottom of the coaster. Because the two fields are attracted to each other, when the motor advances the field along the tracks, the train is pulled right behind. Coasters using this technology can attain speeds of zero to 70 miles (112 km) per hour in less than two seconds! They can stop just as quickly when the polarities of the magnetic fields are reversed, meaning they repel rather than attract each other. This also allows the coaster to run backward as the magnetic field on the track pushes rather than pulls the one on the coaster.

Water-park engineers deal with the same physical principles—gravity, acceleration, resistance—as roller-coaster designers, but instead of engineering the mechanics to pull or push cars over a track, they consider the force of the human body as it moves along a slide. Besides gravity, two main considerations are the friction between the body and the slide and the effects of water as it pushes the body and acts as a lubricant. Engineers also have to think about the force of **inertia**—the body's desire to keep moving—as it banks around curves.

While the basic principles behind water-slide design stay the same, engineers are always thinking of new ways to improve the efficiency, speed, and entertainment value of their rides. The Verrückt waterslide at Schlitterbahn Waterpark in Kansas City is the tallest one in the world. It has an initial drop of more than 168 feet (51.2 m), a hill, and a second drop of 50 feet (15.2 m). To get riders over the second hump, engineers had to design a special nozzle-based system that detects the weight of each raft and blasts enough water to propel it forward. The Mammoth "water coaster" at Holiday World in Indiana uses round boats that hold six riders. The boats are pulled along a track with linear induction motors—the same technology found in modern roller coasters—to dramatically increase speed on both uphill and downhill sections. For the Aqualoop slide in Ixtapan de la Sal, Mexico, engineers had to devise a way for riders to achieve enough speed to make it all the way through a nearly vertical

## Coasting Into the Future

On the design side of roller-coaster development, new software exists that allows engineers to create digital models of their coasters and virtually "test" the ride before construction. Programs from companies like Autodesk® even help engineers see what speeds and gravitational forces will be at various points on the ride, and what the weakest parts of the track are. It also lets them play with all sorts of innovative new designs (like corkscrews and involved loops) without having to commit to construction.

loop. They decided to drop riders through a trapdoor at the start, which enables them to reach speeds of almost 40 miles per hour.

Almost everyone loves the thrills of a water park, but increasing awareness of its environmental impact has forced engineers to incorporate more sustainable designs. Some parks now install special filtration systems to clean their water so they don't have to use harmful chemicals. One park in Wisconsin uses sphagnum moss, commonly known as peat moss, for filtration purposes. This reduces the park's need for chemicals by 90 percent. Sphagnum moss can hold a lot of water; instead of using half a million gallons (1.8 million l) of water per year to cycle through the park, it now only uses 150,000. (567,000 l). Waste water is moss-filtered a second time, recycling 375,000 gallons (1.4 million l) every three months.

## Engineering Behind the Scenes

Even things you don't see—like the signal that brings a television program into your house—require the expertise of an engineer. A broadcast engineer is a special type of electrical engineer who designs, installs, and maintains broadcasting systems for radio and television. Those systems typically begin in a studio. Here, engineers set up equipment, like microphones and cameras, for video or audio programs. The equipment turns sounds and images into electrical signals. In the past, such signals were sent to analog transmitters: electronic devices that changed the signals into radio waves and "transmitted" the waves into the air. On the other end of the system, a radio or television antenna picked up the transmitted waves—and voilà, you had your evening's entertainment.

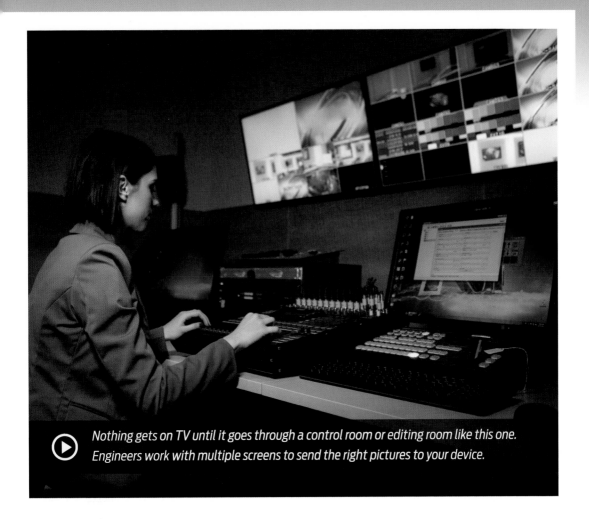

*Nothing gets on TV until it goes through a control room or editing room like this one. Engineers work with multiple screens to send the right pictures to your device.*

In 2009, however, the television broadcasting standard of the United States officially transitioned from analog to digital. Digital signals are not broadcast as radio waves but as pieces of electronic code. Digital antennas, satellites, or cable receiver boxes take this code and convert it for television. Because more information can be sent and received digitally, images and sound come through with greater clarity. Radio is still broadcast in both analog and digital, but digital formats such as HD (high definition) and satellite radio are growing in popularity.

## Engineer of the Movies

Sometimes entertainment meets engineering in less obvious ways. Take the case of Roger Corman, a famous Hollywood producer who happened to have an industrial engineering degree from prestigious Stanford University. Though he did not go on to build any significant physical structures, Corman credited his engineering training with helping him "build" motion pictures. He learned how to plan productions the way engineers plan construction projects, aiming for maximum efficiency and minimum waste. He would often reuse sets from big-budget movies to shoot his own. He worked quickly, sometimes producing up to seven films a year. The mathematical side of his engineering training gave him a head for figures, and he was able to stick closely to his projected budgets for every film.

The changeover to digital has gone hand-in-hand with the rise of the Internet. In fact, more American homes now have Internet connections than high-definition television sets. That means more and more media content is being delivered and consumed through the web. The job of the broadcast engineer has widened—he or she must know about computer networks in addition to broadcasting systems. Broadcast engineers of the future will have to think about integrating smartphones, tablets, and other "mobile receivers" into their systems. They may find themselves part engineer, part information-technology specialist.

## Into "The Void"

Combining the latest in virtual reality (VR) technology with elaborately engineered sets, The Void theme park in Pleasant Grove, Utah, represents the next step in interactive entertainment. At The Void, the user doesn't just sit still and experience the digital worlds depicted on her VR headset—she gets to walk, run, bend down, and reach and grab for objects as she navigates an enormous stage or "arena." In addition, the user experiences the physical sensations of the virtual world, like elevation changes, rises and falls in temperature and air pressure, and the scents of different environments.

While technologists and computer scientists contributed a great deal to the project, engineers were responsible for designing and constructing the physical stage. One of the key features of The Void is the hallway that curves around the perimeter of the space. This was specially designed for a VR concept known as "redirected walking": even when circling around the hallway, the user feels as though he is walking in a straight line. This

At The Void theme park in Utah, visitors become immersed in the environments in which they visit.

© 2015 THE VOID

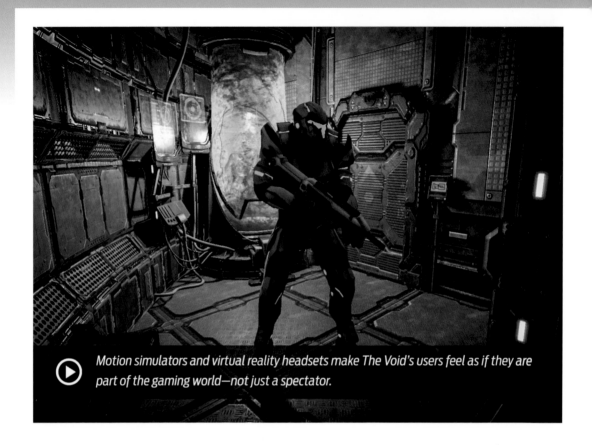

Motion simulators and virtual reality headsets make The Void's users feel as if they are part of the gaming world—not just a spectator.

creates the illusion of covering a great distance, even within a confined space.

Engineers also worked to create a unique two-seat motion simulator. It has a full, 360-degree range of motion, and performs all types of dips, rolls, and side-to-side turns. Coupled with VR headsets, the simulator can create the illusion of being in an aircraft dogfight, a spaceship leaving the atmosphere, or a submarine exploring underwater depths.

Matching the virtual environment with the physical space was a key challenge for The Void's engineers. In one virtual experience, for instance, the user has the option of riding an elevator. To mimic the sensation, engineers constructed a small platform that can move up and down; electric vibrators embedded in the platform add to the effect. Other engineering solutions are a little less involved, such as fans or sprinklers to imitate wind and rain.

# An Engineering Spectacle

The Macy's Thanksgiving Day Parade is a legendary New York tradition. Every year since 1924, the collection of performers, musicians, and fabulous floats has wended its way through the streets of Manhattan. It currently attracts some 3.5 million spectators, with an additional 50 million television viewers, making it the most prominent parade in the country by far.

The highlight of the event remains the massive, helium-filled balloon characters that float above the streets. Everyone from the Pillsbury Doughboy to Snoopy to Shrek has been memorialized in balloon form—some of which are so large they need 90 people to handle them! Creating the memorable balloons not only takes artistic ingenuity, but also a good deal of old-fashioned, nuts-and-bolts engineering. A crew of 28 full-time employees at the Macy's Parade Studio in Moonachie, New Jersey, works year-round to ensure that the spectacle (quite literally) "gets off the ground."

Building anything that's as tall as a five-story building demands the oversight of professionals, and the parade balloons are no different. After an artist renders a pencil sketch of a proposed design, engineers look it over to make sure it is aerodynamic enough to fly. The staff then builds a scale model of the balloon out of clay. From the model, they cast miniature replicas. Engineers study the replicas and note where they should be inflated, where to attach the guide ropes, and other technical concerns. The replicas are then immersed in water; by seeing how much liquid the replicas displace, engineers can calculate the amount of helium gas necessary to keep them afloat. The average balloon needs 12,000 cubic feet (340 cu m) of helium.

*Engineering and science—and people power at the end of all those ropes—combine to keep this massive balloon aloft for the Thanksgiving Day Parade.*

When all this information is compiled, the team is ready to begin building the balloon. The specifications of the replica are imported into a computer to create a digital model. Large pieces of polyurethane fabric are cut and fused to create the balloon. Engineers prefer this fabric to rubber, which the balloons were originally made of. It is more durable, holds its coloring better, and makes the balloons easier to handle.

 ## Text-Dependent Questions

1. How did the engineers behind *Kà* make their set environmentally friendly?

2. How do linear motors work, and in what ways have they changed roller-coaster design?

3. What are some ways the job of a broadcast engineer is changing with the rise of digital media?

 ## Research Project

Look at the radio and/or television in your home. Find out how it receives its signal, what type of signal (analog or digital) it is, and the different components (e.g., antenna, satellite, DVR cable box) the system uses. Research how the broadcast system works for your equipment, then draw a sketch of how programs reach you.

The money comes in to theaters like this one and, after careful accounting, the "box-office" totals for every movie are announced to fans, movie companies, and stars.

# MATH AND
# Entertainment

## Words to Understand

**aesthetically**   relating to ideas of beauty

**algorithms**   step-by-step processes or series of operations used to solve a problem or calculate information

**compile**   to assemble information from various sources

**dispersal**   the action of distributing something

**simulate**   to imitate the appearance of or make a computer reproduction of something

**trigonometry**   a branch of mathematics that focuses on the relationships between triangles

## Math Tracks Sales

At first glance, math and the entertainment industry don't quite seem to go together. We tend to think of numbers and equations as being used in fields such as engineering, finance, or computer science; rarely do we consider that entertainment professionals from cinematographers to animators to bookkeepers all use math to create and produce their projects. Math is also necessary to track the sales of these projects, such as the number of tickets sold for a movie on its opening weekend, so that studios can get a sense of how well something is performing.

The publishing and music industries do this, too, for books and records. The online bookseller Amazon.com uses various **algorithms** to rank sales and make product recommendations. The algorithms **compile** different strands of data. Things like words in the title that people might search for, the book's description

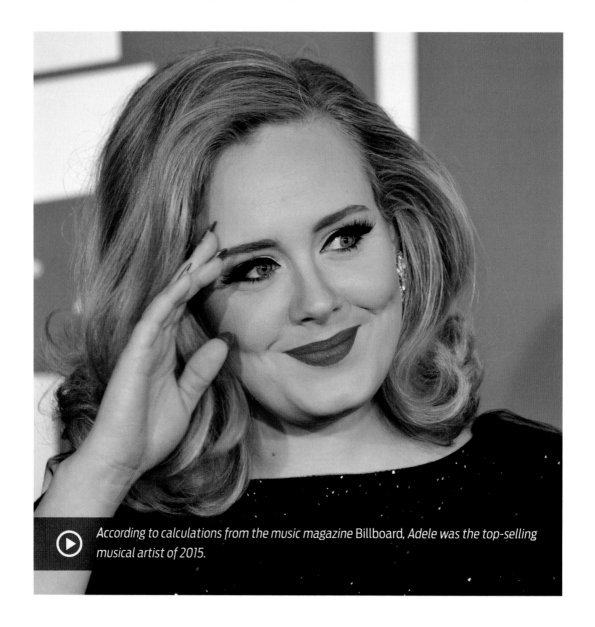

According to calculations from the music magazine Billboard, Adele was the top-selling musical artist of 2015.

and category, and the price and speed of sales are all used to help customers find books and to show which ones are the most popular. There are different algorithms for different sales charts, such as overall bestsellers or top rated within an individual category. Services like Nielsen BookScan gather sales data directly from traditional bookstores and online sellers. They compile this weekly for publication.

Since the 1950s, the music magazine *Billboard* has tracked the sales of songs and albums. For years, lists like the *Billboard* Hot 100 (measuring individual songs) and the Heatseekers chart (measuring albums from newer bands) used physical sales and radio airplay to determine rankings. Technological developments over the past decade, however, have forced *Billboard* to update its approach significantly. Rankings must now account for the number of times a song is downloaded (even as a ringtone), streamed over the Internet or through services like Spotify, and shared through social networking sites. This is known as "multi-platform" or "multi-format" consumption. It has changed sales algorithms completely. Mathematicians working with music industry professionals have come up with new measurements that account for these changes. For instance, 10 digital track sales or 1,500 song streams from an album now equals one album sale.

## Looking for a Hit

Algorithms aren't just used to track sales. They are now being used to analyze songs, film scripts, and other media to predict whether or not they'll be successful. Songwriters can now upload their tunes to a web-based algorithm that measures their "hit potential" by comparing them with past songs. Other companies have produced similar algorithms for the film industry, where studio executives can submit scripts to predict how much they'd make at the box office. Supporters of the technology say that they help find undiscovered artists. Others worry that testing everything with algorithms will limit creativity and make it harder for new, unique voices to be heard.

It isn't just the sales of "finished products" like books or movies that must be tracked. During film shoots, production accountants are responsible for watching over the budgets, making sure that people get paid on time, taking care of day-to-day **dispersal** of cash, preparing reports for the production staff and investors (people putting up the money for the project), and other tasks.

## Counting the Money

All businesses need some sort of accounting, but film is especially difficult because of the often huge budgets involved. It is not uncommon for a studio to set aside $50 million or more to produce a movie. With so much money moving among such large crews, production accountants are often called to perform audits—detailed inspections of financial records—to make sure resources aren't being wasted. They might also help plan a film's budget and speak with investors on behalf of the producer or director.

While accounting methods tend to be pretty similar no matter what the business, new technologies have made them easier and more accessible to all sorts of filmmakers. It used to be that only big-budget movies could afford to hire a professional production accountant. Now, thanks to Internet-based accounting services such as FreshBooks or QuickBooks Online, smaller productions can either do the accounting themselves or hire accounting firms or independent accountants at a fraction of the cost. Instead of having to send an accountant on the road with a film production, the accountant can work from his or her home or office. The film's production team can stay in touch via email and keep the necessary figures up to date.

The movie business is not all glamour and red carpets. Thousands of people work behind the scenes to make sure the math meets the money before anyone can make magic.

## Math Makes Movies

Chapter 1 touched a bit on how physics equations are used to make CGI movies more realistic. But many advanced mathematical concepts like **trigonometry** and integral calculus are also key in rendering CGI scenes. Computer animators must break down very complicated forms—such as the image of a human body—into basic shapes. This way they can "build" digital characters, then animate them.

A single CGI character may have 700 different "controls," or ways of movement. Animators rotate and move characters using principles of trigonometry. To add further detail to characters' motion and shape, animators apply an advanced geometric concept known as harmonic coordinates. Coordinates are values that show the position of a point in space. Points on the surface of the character correspond to points away from the surface. By

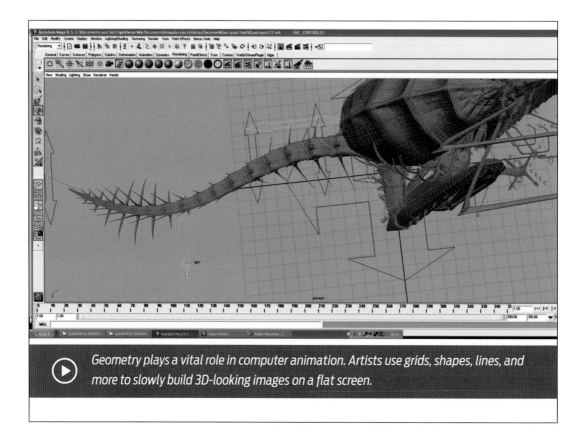

*Geometry plays a vital role in computer animation. Artists use grids, shapes, lines, and more to slowly build 3D-looking images on a flat screen.*

manipulating the relationship between these points, animators can change the shape of the character and simplify the animation process.

After the characters are completed, they are placed in the CGI settings that make them come to life. Math is important for this stage, too. Integral calculus is a branch of math that assembles (or *integrates*) small amounts of something to find out how much there is in total. Animators use it to re-create the effects of multiple light sources coming together at different points. They can then calculate how light changes in an environment to **simulate** its effects within a CGI landscape.

Math isn't limited to CGI movies. Live action films use it as well. Directors compose images with certain geometrical patterns in mind, like the "Rule of Thirds." This is a technique in which an image is divided into thirds both horizontally and vertically. Key elements of the image, such as a person's eyes or the dominant part of a landscape, should appear along the imaginary horizontal or vertical lines. This makes the image more **aesthetically** pleasing. Similar to the Rule of Thirds is the "Golden Mean," a way of organizing an image along the line of a spiral.

Cinematographers and camera operators have to be conscious of math when they calculate shot angles, lens dimensions, and the effects of lens filters and different kinds of film. The distance between the camera's lens and the film itself is called the focal length. It's important that this be accurate for close-up zooms and keeping things in focus. An f-stop is the size of the opening of a lens. The bigger the f-stop, the more light is let into the camera and the brighter the image will be. Getting f-stops to correspond with focal lengths is a big part of a cinematographer's job, and requires a lot of quick-thinking math skills.

Today's digital video cameras are equipped with automatic focus features. The cameraperson can aim the camera at a particular object in the viewfinder, usually framed with a square, and

This digital camera was engineered with a larger viewfinder, so the operator can see how the "shot" is framed. The shoulder harness helps share the load.

MENU

SET

CANCEL

REC    22:08:43:18

A ---min
B 112 min

35 M
1920x1

LAF

A 6400 K  -  +      0000
F3.7   L0.0 dB  1/50

CH1
-dB 4030
CH2

*The screen of a digital video camera provides a wealth of information to the operator, from running time to focus to internal camera settings.*

digital sensors do the rest. Convenient as autofocus is, it sometimes zeroes in on the wrong subject. It might also not work for cinematographers who have a particular shot in mind. Though movies are increasingly shot in digital formats (instead of on film), cinematographers must still use math to compose images, adjust colors, and compress and store files. Regardless of the technology, the rules of physics and math will always apply.

## Editorial Precision

A film editor is someone who takes all the "raw" footage shot for a movie and pieces it together to tell a story. The editor must think mathematically as he or she adds or trims footage to get the movie to a desired length. In the olden days of film, this meant sitting at a large desk called an editing bay and physically cutting and pasting pieces of celluloid film together into strips. Editors knew that 24 frames of film equaled one second of screen time, and they assembled film based on this. Today, this process is done digitally. Computer programs like Final Cut Pro and Media Composer give editors much more control. They can search their footage easily for images or sounds, cut it with greater precision, and add digital effects within the editing process. Timelines beneath the film give them a clearer sense of length as they are working.

*Yes, they do know what all those buttons are for. When editing a film, the editor creates effects, keeps track of changes, and "builds" the final film.*

# Text-Dependent Questions

1. How have recent changes in the music industry changed sales algorithms?

2. What are some branches of higher mathematics used in CGI animations, and what are they used for?

3. How might cinematographers use geometry to compose a shot?

 # Research Project

Using a digital camera, take a series of photographs that demonstrate perspective—that is, where one object is further in the distance than another. What is the relationship between the distance of the object(s) from your camera and their height? Write a brief description of each of your images, identifying how perspective influences the scale of the objects.

More information about CGI technology

# Find Out More

## Books

France, Anna Kaziunas. *Make: 3D Printing: The Essential Guide to 3D Printers*. Sebastopol, Calif: Maker Media, 2014. Everything you ever wanted to know about 3D printing.

## Websites

*Science World Report* is a comprehensive site featuring science-related stories from around the globe.
*www.scienceworldreport.com/*

A widely read periodical on all things science and technology, *Wired* magazine covers the intersection of pop culture and the tech fields.
*www.wired.com*

The Science and Entertainment Exchange, a part of the National Academy of Sciences, "connects entertainment industry professionals with top scientists and engineers," resulting in unique collaborations that benefit everyone.
*www.scienceandentertainmentexchange.org/*

ScienceDaily is a one-stop site for top news stories relating to science, with continually updated information from around the globe.
*www.sciencedaily.com/*

The long-running magazine *Popular Mechanics* hosts a special site for science-related advances in the entertainment industry, which it calls "the science of having fun."
*www.popsci.com/tags/entertainment*

# Series Glossary of Key Terms

**capacity**   the amount of a substance that an object can hold or transport

**consumption**   the act of using a product, such as electricity

**electrodes**   a material, often metal, that carries electrical current into or out of a nonmetallic substance

**evaporate**   to change from a liquid to a gas

**fossil fuels**   a fuel in the earth that formed long ago from dead plants and animals

**inorganic**   describing materials that do not contain the element carbon

**intermittently**   not happening in a regular or reliable way

**ion**   an atom or molecule containing an uneven number of electrons and protons, giving a substance either a positive or negative charge

**microorganism**   a tiny living creature visible only under a microscope

**nuclear**   referring to the nucleus, or center, of an atom, or the energy that can be produced by splitting or joining together atoms

**organic**   describing materials or life forms that contain the element carbon; all living things on Earth are organic

**piston**   part of an engine that moves up and down in a tube; its motion causes other parts to move

**prototype**   the first model of a device used for testing; it serves as a design for future models or a finished product

**radiation**   a form of energy found in nature that, in large quantities, can be harmful to living things

**reactor**   a device used to carry out a controlled process that creates nuclear energy

**sustainable**   able to be used without being completely used up, such as sunlight as an energy source

**turbines**   an engine with large blades that turn as liquids or gases pass over them

**utility**   a company chosen by a local government to provide an essential product, such as electricity

# Index

3D technology 14, 15, 27, 30, 31, 32
accounting 56, 57
acoustics 38
animal handlers 9, 10
Avatar 12
*Billboard* 53
chromakey 22, 23
Cirque de Soleil 30, 35, 36
computer-aided design (CAD) 13, 31
computer-generated imagery (CGI) 12, 13, 23, 56, 57
Corman, Roger 44
dance, science of 16, 17
Dawn of the Planet of the Apes 25
Downey, Robert Jr. 31
green-screen technology 21, 22, 23
Holiday World 41
insect wranglers 9

*Iron Man 2* 31
Macy's Thanksgiving Day Parade 47, 48
Ká 35, 36
Marvel Universe Live! 37
motion-capture technology 24, 25, 26
movie box-office statistics 52, 53
music sales statistics 53
physics 17, 18
rollercoasters 38, 39, 40
"rule of thirds" 57
Sand Cliff Deck 36, 37
Schlitterbahn Waterpark 41
scientific consultants 16
video engineering 42, 43, 44, 58, 59
virtual reality 28, 29
Void, The 44, 45, 46, 47
water parks 40, 41
Wheatstone, Sir Charles 13

# Credits

# About the Author

**Michael Centore** is a writer and editor. He has helped produce many titles, including memoirs, cookbooks, and educational materials, among others, for a variety of publishers. He has authored several previous volumes for Mason Crest, including titles in the Major Nations in a Global World and North American Natural Resources series. His essays have appeared in the *Los Angeles Review of Books*, *Killing the Buddha*, *Mockingbird*, and other print- and web-based publications. He lives in Connecticut.